Cities for the many
not the few

Ash Amin, Doreen Massey and Nigel Thrift

The POLICY
P~P
PRESS

First published in Great Britain in June 2000 by The Policy Press

The Policy Press
University of Bristol
34 Tyndall's Park Road
Bristol BS8 1PY
UK

Tel no +44 (0)117 954 6800
Fax no +44 (0)117 973 7308
E-mail tpp@bristol.ac.uk
www.policypress.org.uk

© The Policy Press, 2000

ISBN 1 86134 258 6

Ash Amin is Professor of Geography at the University of Durham, **Doreen Massey** is Professor of Geography at The Open University and **Nigel Thrift** is Professor of Geography at the University of Bristol.

The right of Ash Amin, Doreen Massey and Nigel Thrift to be identified as authors of this work has been asserted by them in accordance with Sections 77 and 78 of the 1988 Copyright, Designs and Patents Act.

Cover and text design by Dave Worth, University of Bristol
Image used on front cover supplied by kind permission of Steve Russell, Cambridge; cartoon used in text supplied by kind permission of Bill Morrison Photographs used in text supplied by kind permission of Neil Cummings, chanceprojects
Printed in Great Britain by Hobbs the Printers Ltd, Southampton

Contents

Acknowledgements

This document is one product of a year-long discussion among a number of UK urbanists at seminars sponsored by geographers at the Universities of Bristol and Durham and The Open University. We should like to thank each of the departments for their financial help, Michael Pryke of the Geography Department at The Open University for the initiation and overall organisation of the seminars, and Trudy Graham, Kit Kelly and Michele Marsh for their secretarial help.

Participants at the discussions which led to the production of this report were:

John Allen, The Open University

Keith Bassett, University of Bristol

Martin Boddy, University of Bristol

Gary Bridge, University of Bristol

Angus Cameron, University of Durham

Allan Cochrane, The Open University

Mike Crang, University of Durham

Steve Graham, University of Newcastle

Patsy Healey, University of Newcastle

Steve Hinchliffe, The Open University

Ray Hudson, University of Durham

Roger Lee, Queen Mary & Westfield College

Ali Madanipour, University of Newcastle

Linda McDowell, University College London

Joe Painter, University of Durham

Adrian Passmore, The Open University

Steve Pile, The Open University

Michael Pryke, The Open University

Jenny Robinson, The Open University

David Sadler, University of Durham

John Solomos, South Bank University

Alan Townsend, University of Durham

Sophie Watson, University of East London

Sarah Whatmore, University of Bristol

Preface

Cities are the focus of much of our national life. They are, we believe, cradles of creativity – economically, culturally, socially and politically. They are also, of course, the locus of many of our most well-rehearsed national problems. And, for reasons which we shall elaborate, they also pose some of the toughest challenges to (and perhaps best hopes for) democracy.

It is right, then, that cities are a focus of government policy. Labour's return to power in 1997 heralded a long-overdue recognition of the centrality of cities in national economic, social and cultural life. The government saw the sense of making cities more liveable and sustainable, reducing social polarisation and exclusion within them and improving their economic potential. Indeed, there are journalists who report that "the great task of reviving Britain's cities and towns may be Number 10's 'big idea' for the next election" (Marr, *The Observer,* 12 March 2000).

To approach something as complex as policy for cities it is necessary to have a framing *vision*: of what and who cities are for, and what kinds of societies they might most democratically embody. What we aim to do here is to reflect on that wider vision. This is not a document about the detail of policy interventions (although we believe that also to be extremely important). Rather it seeks to pose bigger questions about how we might imagine cities for the new century.

New Labour policy on cities is still in the making. So this document is partly an assessment of what has been proposed so far, and partly a proposal for what else might be imagined. Enough has already emerged from the government, however, to make it clear that our vision is different on two fundamental counts.

First: the question of the *economy*. The government sees urban economic regeneration (outside the nation's most deprived neighbourhoods) in the context of a global shift towards a knowledge economy based on intangible goods, information and communication technologies and knowledge workers. We argue that the transition to the knowledge economy has yet to be proven and that the urban economic mainstream – in and beyond the knowledge economy – will continue to require traditional resources such as caterers, cleaners, tangible goods, part-time and seasonal work, and age-old means of communication. Knowledge-driven competitiveness will not magic away these aspects of the labour market. Moreover, an exclusive emphasis on 'the knowledge economy' in the way New Labour typically defines it stands to have problematic social effects. It assumes an upward drift in class allegiance, at the expense of the mass of ordinary citizens who make up cities.

Second: the question of *democracy.* The currently available government thoughts on city policy point to a number of agents in addition to central and local government as key to urban transformation. In some, the entrepreneurial and professional middle classes are the focus, in others the prevailing tenor is one of moral authoritarianism, in yet others there are calls for (and real attempts at) community participation, usually around particular projects, and usually on behalf of the most deprived. Some of this is appealing, some distinctly less so. Many of the government-inspired innovations (such as, for example, the New Opportunities funded from Chris Smith's department, or its Active Community Demonstration Projects which aim to monitor public involvement in community life in five boroughs) are potentially excellent in their own right. But there is no overall conception of 'urban citizenship' within which all this can be set. One issue about democracy concerns the need for a systematic inclusiveness. We need a strategy for urban democracy that seeks to empower across the social spectrum and which feels comfortable with the reconstruction of cities as a plural and open-ended process.

This raises a further crucial issue. And that is that cities, maybe in general but certainly in Britain today, pose questions about the very form of democracy and public 'participation'. They do this in two ways. Firstly cities vary: in their needs, their potential, their social character. They are the seedbeds for an assertion of the energy of 'the local'. Correspondingly they are a challenge to any government with tendencies towards a centralisation of control over politics yet with devolution of power to cities and urban mayors as one of its commitments. Secondly cities are essentially culturally hybrid and inevitably conflictual. This is part of their creative character and their dynamism. There is simply no point in imagining the future of cities in terms of a harmonious, consensual, 'solution' – a 'state' which can be arrived at. What we need are mechanisms for ensuring the democratic control and management of what will necessarily, by the very nature of cities, be a constantly contested, constantly changing, open future.

***

The vision offered in this document argues for economic and democratic reforms centred around the daily and ordinary aspects of urban living. It begins from the premiss that even the knowledge economy so desired by the government will require the provision of what many would consider old sorts of jobs and welfare. And it argues that we need to have confidence in the power of active citizenship across the social and class spectrum.

New Labour currently has a plethora of initiatives relevant to cities, and contributions to urban change are developed in a range of departments. The task of tackling social exclusion was entrusted to the various urban regeneration programmes run from the Department of the Environment, Transport and the Regions (DETR) and the Social Exclusion Unit tied to Number 10. The government's White Paper to be published later this year will add economic policy measures. In many ways this multi-faceted character is sensible, as is its experimental nature. However, the number of pilot programmes verges on the bewildering. Quite apart from the pressures which must be imposed on those at the sharp end, trying to implement government policy, this scattergun approach poses two problems which are central to our argument here. To begin with it is potentially divisive. As Angus Cameron (personal communication) notes: we have Rogers on the 'urban', the Social Exclusion Unit on poor 'neighbourhoods' and the local government White Paper on local 'governance'. The consequence of this is to provide one set of policies for the urban middle classes, one for the urban poor, and another for the partial reform of the political establishment governing both. Moreover, as Peck and Theodore (1999) have argued in the context of the New Deal, New Labour are policy pragmatists, creating numerous experiments, often on a reactive basis. This is the antithesis of policy driven by vision.

Yet amidst all this one major report has emerged which does indeed embody an urban vision. This is *Towards an urban renaissance*, the report of the Urban Task Force chaired by Lord Rogers. Although the Rogers Report (1999a) is one strand of an evolving urban policy domain, with a specific mission to ground urban regeneration in "design excellence, social well-being and environmental responsibility", it draws on as distinctive and comprehensive a vision as any of the 'good' city. It is because we believe that this kind of breadth of imagination is necessary that we begin from the Rogers Report. We examine the Report in the next chapter. The following chapters outline our own understanding of cities, and take up in turn the question of the economy and the question of democracy.

© Bill Morrison

The Rogers Report:
Towards an urban renaissance

Richard Rogers' Report is wonderfully enthusiastic about cities and their potential. It makes proposals which aim to reverse the urban rot and flight encouraged by the market-driven policies of the previous Conservative administrations. It laments the under-investment, urban shabbiness, sprawl, congestion and pollution encouraged by the legacy of US-inspired policies on cities. It looks instead to thriving European cities such as Amsterdam and Barcelona for a model of the safe, sustainable and human-scale city that offers plenty of scope for work, play and habitability. Thus, the opening page of the Executive summary of the Report proclaims:

> Towns and cities should be well designed, be more compact and connected, support a range of diverse uses within a sustainable urban environment. [...] The process of change should combine strengthened democratic local leadership with an increased commitment to public participation. (Urban Task Force, 1999b, p 1)

The Report recommends the reclamation of derelict and vacant urban land and buildings – existing brownfield conversion – in order to regain urban density. It prioritises compact, mixed-use developments, pedestrianised zones, public transport, and cycle routes in order to halt the car craze supported by the last government. It recommends a national campaign to improve urban design and restore architecture and planning in general. And it argues that the delivery of this agenda should be centred around the local authorities, with the support of planning professionals and community organisations, especially in "council estates and other depressed neighbourhoods" (Urban Task Force, 1999b, p 5).

There is much here to be welcomed.

In the wake of a long history of English anti-urbanism, the positive tone on urban possibility is overdue. Against the commonly held ✗ dystopian view of cities as sources of economic, social and environmental decline, the 90% of England's population who live and work in the urban areas are promised a better future, based on, "the principles of design excellence, social well being and environmental responsibility within a viable economic and legislative framework" (Task Force's mission statement).

Again, after the last government's cult of US-inspired models of urban regeneration, the Rogers Report comes as a breath of fresh air. It is timely that the dominance of US influence on city policy – predicated on market selection or abandonment of particular groups and zones in cities – is counter-balanced by a more positive West European vision of cities as sources of economic and social well-being, cultural mixture and citizenship.

It is also right that the Report, significantly, rejects the Conservative legacy of decision making through central government, unelected quangos, and business luminaries. Rogers envisages a model of urban governance which includes opening up planning decisions to neighbourhood actors, creating neighbourhoods with mixed tenure and incomes, strengthening the strategic and executive powers of local authorities, targeting Urban Priority Areas for speedy regeneration by private–public companies, and building local capacity in urban management skills. After years of Conservative neglect, the recognition of the public sector, democratic legitimacy, and the needs of the most disadvantaged groups and neighbourhoods is to be applauded.

© Neil Cummings, courtesy of chanceprojects

The focus on environmental sustainability, and the recognition that cities are not the antithesis to nature, and the support for public transport as against cars, the consideration of waste-management and so forth all have the potential to open up a debate about the ecology of cities which is sorely needed.

And the enthusiasm for design itself is important. The physical look and feel of our surroundings has an effect. Davis (1998) has demonstrated clearly the intimate relations between architecture and power, the deeper meanings of the private enclosures of affluence, the surveillance of public space. Many of the details of Rogers' design suggestions, as well as some of the bigger ones, could make, if implemented, a big difference to our lives.

There is a host of other ways, too, in which the Report is to be welcomed. The attention to housing, the recognition of traditionally low-status services, a call to consider the mobility of elderly people. If New Labour is actually able to act on all these recommendations, our cities might be considerably improved.

***

And yet ... there are aspects of this vision which are nonetheless inadequate as a basis for reimagining urban policy.

First, and even given its brief, the Report offers an overly design-led urban vision. Although the Report is quick to stress that urban social and economic problems require further action beyond "solution by design", nonetheless the centrality of this document to the government's set of projects, and the overwhelming tenor of the Report itself, give cause for concern.

The reason for concern is that there is a history to all this. Putting the design of the physical fabric first is reminiscent of the urban environmental determinism of the 1960s, when local coalitions of planners, architects and local government officials – in good faith – plastered roads, housing estates and concrete in general over the cracks of working-class urban deprivation. It is also curiously reminiscent of the Tory years, when local coalitions of property developers, business executives and development corporations – in blithe contempt of work and welfare – face-lifted city centres, warehouses, waterfronts, and derelict spaces as sites of consumption, play, spectacle and magnets for investment. The (very welcome) difference is that now the city is imagined for mixed uses and mixed actors, but the confidence in the powers of urban design(ers), bricks and mortar, and the transport and communications infrastructure remains undiminished.

Second, there is an underlying presupposition of an attainable urban harmony. Rogers' new compact city will strike a balance between nature, built environment and society, between private, public and community, between work, travel, home, shopping and play. This harmony is based on a rose-tinted evocation of the centres of selected European cities – their historical architecture, busy markets, small shops, cafes and squares, mixed buildings and residential blocks and proud citizens. But harmony in this sense is actually the last thing cities are about. The imagery evoked, while undoubtedly an ideal, bears no resemblance to current urban realities in Britain nor, more importantly given the Report's models, to most European outer-city areas. But more than that, the essentially conflictual and contested nature of cities is not confronted. 'The public realm' is too often evoked as a neutral space where all can come together unproblematically. Yet we know this not to be the case. Public space at its worst can be the site of one group's dominance over others. At its best it can be a place of active engagement and debate. The city is a place of difference, and that includes different interests. A policy which does not square up to that will not address the underlying problems. The quiet harmony of interests which seems to be an underlying assumption of much of the Rogers Report has, interestingly, much in common with New Labour's notion of a 'big tent'. By ignoring the real conflicts of interest, the occasional zero-sum game, it fails to address the issue of power.

Third, and relatedly, there is a whole side of cities which seems to be missing here. In part there is a lack of recognition of the sheer variety of urban experience. The vibrancy of urban life, bringing as it does diversity in close proximity, is certainly about creative intermingling, cultural mixture, and exploratory potential. But for many it is also about the desperate search for privacy, sanctuary and anonymity, about coping with loneliness, fear and anxiety, about being seen, heard and recognised, about jostling for space, work and welfare, about resentment, anger and intolerance. In part there is an absence in this Report of ethnicity, and of the general mixity of cities. And in part there is an absence of what we might call the underground or unseen city: not just the illegality but the car-boot sale, the huge networks of hobby groups, the myriad of everyday activities....

One report, especially one focused on design, could not, of course, be expected to include everything, but if this document is to be as central to the government's projects as it currently seems, then such absences must be noted.

Fourth, we need to confront more directly the dynamism of cities, the forces which are constantly producing change within them. For example, the notion of urban villages of socially and sectorally mixed use (Urban Task Force, 1999a, pp 64-5) is extremely attractive, but how will they be maintained in a context where people change jobs frequently? (There is an assumption that "a growing proportion of urban residents will work in the neighbourhood in which they live" [p 65]). A policy for cities has also to be about both harnessing and confronting the social forces which make cities what they are and through which they are forever changing.

2

Imagining cities

So, what *are* cities? Or, more precisely, how might we conceptualise them in a way that can give us some purchase (a) on the new issues and challenges which are arising at the turn of the millennium and (b) on approaches to policy formulation which might be an adequate response to this new world?

To reconceptualise cities we must draw on some of the recent thinking in the social sciences and humanities. This addresses such issues as:

- ◢ the changing nature of the relation between locality and community in an age of globalisation;
- ◢ the revolution in the way we live our identities, as citizens and members of a society, in an increasingly urbanised, multiple, and interconnected world;
- ◢ the seismic shift in the nature of political identification and participation;
- ◢ the erosion of agreed foundations and certainties about the way society should be organised;
- ◢ the heightened awareness of the significance of spatiality in the organisation of our lives.

These are (some of) the significant changes which we must address; and we may begin by noting that they are in stark contrast to many of the old saws which have, unfortunately, so frequently been taken up as mantras by certain elements of what passes for 'new' thinking. We dispute the claim, for instance, that the all-too-easy references to 'flexibility', 'the knowledge economy', 'weightlessness' and so on are either sufficiently well-grounded empirically or intellectually or practically robust enough really to face up to the challenges which lie ahead (see Chapter 3).

So, given that, how might we imagine cities?

First, let us lay down a general principle: that we intend to define cities in terms of processes and interactions, rather than in terms of 'things'. We want to begin with cities as social arenas rather than as built environments. This means initially imagining cities not, say, as high-rise centres surrounded by suburbs, as parks and roads and municipal buildings, but as interlocking processes of living, meeting, making, relating. This does not mean that we believe the built environment is not significant: far from it. But it does mean that we believe that a 'design-centred solution' is not the best way forward. What matters within cities – what lends them both their problems and their possibilities – revolves around the fact that they are places of social interaction.

Second, there are certain things about 'cities-as-places-of-interaction' which mark them out as distinct, and which help us begin to capture what is specific about the sociability of 'citiness'. Let us begin with two elements:

- cities are particularly *intense* networks of social interaction: probably the characteristic which most distinctively marks out cities as cities is the geographical intensity of social relations and activities which they bring together;

- cities are *meeting places*: they are places where different cultures and life-styles come together geographically: are juxtaposed; where, crucially, they have to find some means of accommodation, the negotiation of difference is even more marked – and even more of a challenge – in cities than it is in other areas.

Both of these characteristics have effects, but neither of them leads to inevitable outcomes. Thus, the intensity of cities can be both unbearable and exciting; their characteristic of juxtaposing diversity can make them (what they often are) the sources of creative activity, the crucibles of the new, or it can engender violence, intercommunal antagonism, and fear. This production of effects which are not determinate can be seen in different spheres of city life. In the economic sphere, for instance, the intensity of cities can generate either the positive externalities of agglomeration or the stifling costs of congestion. Culturally it can generate new cross-overs or walled-in separate communities of mutual suspicion.

This is the paradox of cities: they can be the hope of the future or the dystopia of despair. The policy question is how we take hold of these paradoxical characteristics and build on them in such a way as best to draw out their positive potential.

***

So, let us relate this specificity of cities, as we have defined it so far, to some of the bigger issues – mentioned above – on the wider social canvas:

▶ On the one hand cities are places of the juxtaposition of diversity … and on the other hand intensified globalisation is disrupting and questioning the once-accepted relation between locality and community. Together these facts pose fundamental questions about the social geography of the 21st century city. We are reorganising the way we connect our belonging to a community (usually communit*ies* – see below) and our belonging to a place. Questions of differential power and the functioning of democracy must be central to how we think this through. A 'specialised' area (an ethnic minority community, a 'gay village') can be a way for a group to establish or maintain an identity and to have a voice in a democratic urban debate. But such separation can also be an expression of power *over* others, and of exclusivity (a gated community of the rich, for example). Or, differently again, the spatial concentrations which mark 'sink estates' can be expressions of the, totally opposite, relations of exclusion. How are community and difference to be composed in the internal geography of the city of the future? What is the meaning of 'community' in such a context? Are communities necessarily spatial?

▶ Moreover we live our 'identities' in different ways these days. An individual is likely more explicitly now to see themselves as belonging to more than one community – class, sexual preference, ethnic affiliation…. We may, likewise, connect into the sphere of 'the political' in a multitude of ways. This is not a question of the disintegration of the political into 'single issue politics' – for there are few (so-called) 'single issues' which do not link to a wider politics or connect to another campaign, another 'community'. At the most general level, the policy challenge is how to produce a city within which it is possible to negotiate these increasingly interlocking notions of difference, and a city which is capable of nurturing, and coping with, political participation in such a complexity.

▶ This issue is further complicated by the recognition of another aspect of our political identities. It is not just that the nature of political identification has become looser (the oft-repeated assertion that 'class' is less important, etc). Far more significant than this is the fact that political identifications are not somehow rigidly pre-given in alignment with *any* such characteristics. Rather, political identifications and political constituencies are continually formed and re-formed as issues arise and in the process of political debate and negotiation. This makes it even more vital that access to channels of political/social communication are not restricted to professional politicians, an elite, or the already powerful. It demands a democratic opening of the means of political debate themselves.

▶ And we must push this argument yet one step further. The combination of the diversity of cities with the erosion of certainties about the way society is to be organised means two things. First, it means that in a democratic society everything is up for debate, including the terms of the (necessary) processes of our socialisation – the ways in which we understand society to hang together. Second, it means that the vision of harmony and order (such as that held out by Rogers, and even more by Tony Blair) is not simply unattainable in practice; it is also undemocratic in intent. A modern democracy, and this is *a fortiori* so in the intense diversity of cities, will always be a place of contestation. It will always be 'messy', if you like, but that is part of what gives it life.

***

Third, there are further characteristics of cities – not particular to them (that is, not defining *of* cities) – but characteristics which must be at the forefront of our minds as we approach policy formulation:

▶ *Cities are essentially dynamic* (a characteristic far more readily recognised when we think of them in terms of processes and interactions). Policy formulation must work with this; it must not think in terms of some final, formal plan, nor work with an assumption of a reachable permanent harmony or peace. The order of cities is a dynamic – and frequently conflictual – order. A new politics for cities must be equally fluid and processual. On the one hand this means that the *mechanisms* of city politics will be of supreme importance. Getting the channels and means of democratic decision making right is as important as any particular decision itself. The central issue is that of democratic political empowerment. And the processes of debate and decision making must strive for a fluidity and continuity which reflect the ongoing dynamism of the city itself. On the other hand it means that proposals for specific policies (eg 'urban villages') must be evaluated dynamically (how will they be formed? how can they reproduce themselves over time? will those processes build on and reinforce division and inequality? and so forth).

© Neil Cummings, courtesy of chanceprojects

▶ *Cities are open and interconnected.* This has always been the case and is *a fortiori* so today in the context of intensified globalisation. Again, this is something which is in some ways recognised in much 'new' writing and policy formulation about cities. But the depth and scope of this recognition is usually extremely limited – limited, for instance, to such things as 'competitiveness' between cities. Even this frequently reduces to tautology and is rarely considered 'politically'– the politics of the terms on which places compete against each other is something which needs seriously to be addressed. But there are also other issues. The openness of cities raises, for instance, challenging questions about how to relate the 'global roles' for which all cities appear to be striving to issues of local benefits and accountabilities. This is even more the case because a city will in fact be open to a whole range of global interconnections which will relate to different groups within it. The implication is both that there is usually a greater variety of potential global roles open to a city than is often recognised, and that decisions about which of these roles to prioritise will have social and distributional implications. Becoming a 'global financial centre' can often have effects on the rest of a city's economy (through land prices and distributional implications) which are regressive in terms of any aim of equality. Striving to become 'a city of culture' immediately raises questions of whose culture, in a city which will inevitably bring together, in terms of for instance ethnicity and class, more than one culture. Or again, it is often overlooked that cities can in no way be considered closed systems in policy terms – how this might be recognised is a conundrum which has only very rarely been addressed by urban policy makers, but it is raised, for instance, by the whole notion of a city's 'footprint': a term that is suggestive of the need to understand cities as extending beyond the land-use boundaries that are discerned from aerial photographs. For contemporary interconnected cities, footprints are made up of all manner of links, paths and relations that can be turned on and off, or whose nature can be questioned. There is plenty of evidence that inhabitants of cities are well aware of these interdependencies and the responsibilities that attend to them. Is it too much to ask that there should be a city politics that begins to take these responsibilities seriously (even though this may involve consideration of those who are not part of, and will in all likelihood remain outside of, the city's electorate)? There is a fundamental issue here: how to balance local control with responsible recognition of interdependence.

▶ *Cities are 'spatial' phenomena.* At one level this is plainly evident; and indeed much city planning in the past might reasonably be criticised for having been *too* preoccupied with geographical form. But this is not what we have in mind. Rather, we want to take more seriously the way in which the geographical organisation of a city may be instrumental in producing effects: social, economic, cultural, political. We have already pointed to how this may be the case with the very intensity and juxtaposed diversity of cities; geographical organisation is also evidently an important stake in the relationship between communities, in all their changing forms, within the city. Space and power are intimately interconnected. All spaces embody power relations of some sort – even so-called public spaces (urban parks, for instance) are more 'accessible' (in many tangible and intangible ways) to some groups (and at different times of day and night) than others (see Comedia, 1995). There are countless issues of the differential safety of places to members of the urban population. And inequalities of mobility just have to be one of *the* major issues in imagining and creating the city of the new millennium. (Just one example: a humane, more egalitarian city, would transform the possibilities for mobility of elderly people over what exists at the moment – and 'elderly people' are soon to be the largest age-group in society.) As they are at the moment, cities are riven by exclusions (imposed not by law but by custom, by hostility, by social convention, by difficulty of physical access...); claims on the spaces of cities reflect the differential power of social groups and the constant, and frequently conflictual, negotiation between them. What we are suggesting is that the manner of this social construction of the spaces of the city be more openly and explicitly addressed.

▶ *Cities are not the opposite of 'nature'.* We often tend to think of cities as somehow separate from nature: indeed they are frequently characterised as the opposite of 'nature'. We would question this on the grounds that environmental politics are as pressing in cities as anywhere else. This can be thought of in three senses. First, and most obviously, city environments have effects on health and well-being. Following on from this, differences in environmental quality are a highly significant form of inequality. Likewise, environmental improvements in one area of a city, or one particular city, can be bought at the cost of environmental degradation elsewhere. Related to this is our second sense of urban environmental politics. Cities are, as we have already highlighted, related to a host of other environments through their interconnections. Cities are major sites for the consumption of environmental goods (including water, clean air and so on) and the production of environmental problems. Thought of in this way, cities are locked into, and major players in, resource economies and ecologies. To intervene in these economies requires that we incorporate cities into a broader understanding of environmental processes. Third, and perhaps less obviously, cities are not simply inhabited by human beings. They are also temporary and permanent homes and passageways for an incredible range of other living organisms. In some senses, cities have become important sites for ecological diversity, innovation and evolution. That such ecological value often includes close relationships to human beings should in no way be used to diminish its importance. We should tread carefully, therefore, when we tend to value urban space only for its development potential. As we have said, the Rogers Report goes a long way towards opening up these issues. They should be taken further.

▶ *Cities vary.* Cities have different histories and will have different futures. This is true even within the small context of Britain. It does not mean that there are not some general principles which can apply across the board (that is what this paper is all about). But it does mean, first, that cities should actively cultivate and draw on their own individualities; in particular they should be wary of too easily adopting off-the-shelf policies which are replicated in city after city. As we have seen many times, policy fashions are frequently (precisely as a result of being fashions) self-defeating. Second, each city is a distinctive node in the wider arena of globalised relations. In the UK the clearest difference is between London and other cities. London is a 'world city'. It (or part of it) and its region have off-shore roles in some ways quite distinct from those of other cities. London is also the seat of national power and policy making, and that policy making responds more often to conditions in London and its region than to conditions in other cities. This is an issue which must be taken seriously.

3

The 'new' urban economy

The government's thinking about the future of the urban engine room of the British economy certainly sees cities as becoming more dynamic and cosmopolitan. But that dynamism and cosmopolitanism is a muted rendering of the latest version of the American dream – the knowledge economy. It is a dream in which British cities are able to hitch a ride on the leading edge of an American high-tech capitalism as "the generation and exploitation of knowledge has come to play the predominant part in the creation of wealth" (DTI, 1998, p 3). But even some of the most ardent fans of 'the new economy' doubt whether the market – driven through cities or elsewhere – can provide all the goods.

> The fact that knowledge is, in many ways, a public good and that there are important externalities means that exclusive or excessive reliance on the market may not result in economic efficiency. For those of us who believe in the power of market forces, the challenge is to find the best 'partnership' between the private and public sector – an assignment of roles and responsibilities not dictated by the paradigms of the past that are unsuited to the knowledge economy of the future. (Stiglitz, 1999, p 54)

Our concern is that the dream of a future in which British cities become outposts of the global knowledge economy will only work partially and selectively. And even if that dream were able to be initiated in a few British cities, many of the inhabitants of both those cities and those excluded altogether might find themselves pushed even further into the economic periphery. Whose knowledge? Not theirs.

All that is solid melts into air

So what is this shiny dream that British cities are to be caught up in? It is a dream of a future 'new economy' which will spin knowledge into ever more saleable commodities, producing new times, a new epoch of history in which everything is in continual flux, in which the modern is being continually modernised, in which all that is solid melts into air (eg Quah, 1997; Leadbeater, 1999). Welcome to a new industrial revolution realised through a series of all but inevitable processes:

▶ *Globalisation:* the global market spreads out and becomes more interconnected through the economic processes of multi-national corporations.

▶ *New forms of corporate organisation:* 'fast' networked, non-hierarchical forms of corporate organisation will appear, replacing slow hierarchical, highly bureaucratic organisations. They will allow easier collaboration and easier sharing of knowledge, which, in turn, will mean that these organisations will be able to innovate more easily and act as a buffer against economic strains, since they are more adaptable.

▶ *New working practices:* spurred on by the need for more knowledgeable workers, new working practices evolve. Most especially, work careers become more uncertain so that people must provide for constant changes of job by constantly learning new skills. And, at work, people will become involved in more flexible job situations, able to move from one task to another at times which suit consumers' increasingly 24-hour attention span.

▶ *Information and communication technologies:* these technologies will become pervasive, leading to a complete makeover of the conduct of business and the business of consumption. We have reached the point where these technologies have 'bedded in' and will produce enormous boosts to productivity through new practices like e-commerce.

▶ *Intangible goods:* many modern goods, like software or gene-based new technology, are 'weightless'. That is, they bring producers and consumers much closer together and require very little intermediate structure ('weight') – like transport and shops – to do so. Therefore they behave rather like knowledge itself.

➤ *Clustering:* industries will increasingly cluster in a frenzied search
for interdependencies they are unable to get at a distance. Spatial
contiguity will provide knowledge of what's going on, ability to set
up collaboration, ways of building trust.

If this tidal wave of change splashing over our world and sweeping all
before it seems to be a familiar story, it is because one of the things that
is being retailed is a habit of thinking: the idea that history is a pageant
of grand revolutions in production that we have to adjust to. This
time, a new spectral form of production is having a ghostly party –
and we have to join in. Well, maybe.

For these kinds of epochal accounts of revolutions in history really
ought to give us pause. They rely on exaggeration. In order to make
a point, the point is stretched. To begin with, they assume that change
is inevitable and that the costs of not going along for the ride are
unbearably high. Then, epochal accounts of history must assume that
everything adds up. All the different things going on are playing to
the same tune. A new economy is coming together which we can
unproblematically see, feel and name. Then, they assume that there is
no alternative. The change is going to happen and we need to do
something *now* or we will miss it. Often, measures will then be taken
which not only confirm its existence but may even create parts of it.
And, last, they are in the exaggeration business. In these days of the
archetypal middle-class professional – the management consultant –
exaggeration sells.

None of this is to suggest that nothing new is happening but, as
geographers, we can never see change as a unitary process writ from
on high. Rather, change is a patchwork of processes which cohere in
different ways in different places and so is constantly mutating. Change
is never a single stamp on prepared ground. Rather, change is a dance,
and each of the steps has at least the potential to go off in new directions
as it negotiates all kinds of places, sometimes moving smoothly through
them, sometimes tripping up and having to invent corrections which
may take the dance in entirely different directions.

We can draw three lessons from this point. One is to be very sceptical
of the idea that a process happens equally everywhere. It never does.
The next lesson is to be very suspicious of the use of the prefix 'new'.
It is often used simply to point change in the direction the writer
likes. Equally, it is important to be suspicious of the use of the prefix
'old'. It is often deployed to suggest that some issues and areas are not
worth bothering about – 'old' (and useless) industries, 'old' (and boring)

jobs, 'old' (and out-of-date) technologies, old (and irrelevant) industrial relations. The parts of an economy that do not fit the story of a change to 'the new' are conveyed into the dustbin of history. And the final lesson comes from asking why anyone would want to make these claims in the first place. What is certain is that such claims are rarely disinterested. More often than not they are stories produced by the powerful for the powerful.

Take the case of the six changes in the economy we have noted above, which are all supposed to have enormous impacts on cities and city populations:

- ▶ *Globalisation:* experts cannot even agree on a suitable definition of this phenomenon, let alone its exact extent. While it seems hard to deny the increasing interconnection of the world's economies, this is not the same as arguing that we are moving towards a world in which everything is connected up. Moreover, rather than just taking globalisation as a given, the really serious policy questions should concern the form that it will take (the terms on which it is to be constructed) and, in the context of this discussion, the role that different cities might play within it.

- ▶ *Networked organisations:* the networked, non-hierarchical organisation is hardly ever found in a pure form. Rather it represents an aspiration. What does exist is a host of hybrid forms of organisation, some of which – and not necessarily the most successful – bear the stamp of non-hierarchical organisation. There do, in fact, seem to be many organisational paths to economic success.

- ▶ *New working practices:* again, these are not as new or as widespread as sometimes made out. Evidence for a massive change in career structure, with more and more people changing jobs, is hard to find, except among elites where demand exceeds supply. Similarly, flexible working practices on closer inspection often prove to be much older forms of working practices (like shift systems and home working) with a modern gloss.

- ▶ *Information and communication technologies:* clearly, these technologies are having important effects. But the fact is that nearly all of the effects that are mooted are the subjects of debate. Remember 'the paperless office'? Whether these techniques engender higher production, are able to produce revolutions in production and marketing, are changing our perceptions of time and space: all are at issue. But one thing we can be sure of. They will not be a panacea. They will bring new opportunities but they will also bring new problems.

▶ *Intangible goods:* again, while there are clearly changes under way, it is important not to exaggerate their spread or significance. Many so-called intangible goods are not intangible; rather their materiality is of a different kind from what has gone before, still involves work and is crucially dependent on new kinds of property rights.

▶ *Clustering:* the importance of industrial clustering may be constantly proclaimed but the evidence for success is difficult to interpret. For example, what counts as a cluster is crucial and, crucially, difficult to judge. More than this, most clusters seem to be transitory and their strengths are difficult to maintain. In any case, where they have been successful engines of local economic development, it is because of strong interdependencies among and between local firms and business organisations (ie economies of 'association'), not agglomeration alone. Further, the reasons behind any tendency to cluster need to be examined with care. Many clusters are the product (or partly the product) of rivalry, of follow-my-leader strategies, or of a kind of 'class politics of location' where certain districts are deemed to have a greater status or cachet. Such clustering processes have little to do with any deeper 'economic rationality'.

In other words, practically all of what is currently regarded as new and modern in conventional wisdom may be rather less important than often stated or much more contingent. Given this, we will offer our own account of what is going on behind the re-imaging of British urban economic futures.

The gentrification of the economy?

In 1996 Tony Blair declared "our task is to allow more people to become middle class. The Labour Party did not come into being to celebrate working class people having a lack of opportunities and poverty, but to take them out of it" (*Sunday Times*, 1 September 1996, cited in Adonis and Pollard, 1997). It may well be that parts of British cities are currently being either taken over or at least influenced by the expanding 'middling classes'. Some of the jobs currently being created in British cities are in fast-growing industries like information technology, financial services, various forms of consultancy service and the media, which are the preserve of the middle class and, as importantly in certain respects, they symbolise the new knowledge economy that urban policy makers are so keen to see more of. We also agree that class has changed. 'Classes' today are more fluid, complex, geographically mobile, and cross-cut by other forms of allegiance. Moreover, the middling classes often tend to have a more individualised view of the world which fluidity, mobility and heterogeneity confirm. This has a good side in the general lack of deference and the general expansion of horizons that goes with it. But it also has a downside in that it tends to lead to a model of self-entrepreneurialism – the brand of 'you' – which can in turn encourage a moral minimalism.

Some of the changes to which Blair refers and aspires are, then, occurring. However, we would argue that the middling strata, and the demand for their services in the labour market, are still only one element of the urban population. For example, vacancy data available from the National Online Manpower Information Survey (NOMIS) provides sobering evidence of the kinds of jobs for which there has been demand since the early 1990s. Across the British metropolitan spectrum – in both thriving and older industrial cities – the economy still continues to demand clerical and secretarial workers, personal service providers, sales staff, plant machinery operators and unskilled workers ('elementary occupations'). In any given year, these jobs account for around 70% of notified vacancies in cities such as London, Bristol, Birmingham, Cambridge, Manchester, Newcastle upon Tyne, Edinburgh, Glasgow and Cardiff. Are these the jobs of the fast-moving new economy of networked organisations, clusters of competitive advantage, intangible goods and the Internet? Doubtful. In other words the actual occupational structure is far more complex than New Labour's analysis allows and we have to enquire as to who gets to define the economy in this way, and why.

The answer is that New Labour's 'new economy' is being built around certain class strata, and is producing a world full of the concerns of these strata; concerns like entrepreneurship, self-actualisation, achieving balance between the pressures of work and other commitments, and displaying qualities of leadership and creativity (concerns that are perceived as new, but only because of who they are now affecting: the difficulty of balancing home and work has for a long time been the lot of working-class women!). And there is a corresponding geography

© Neil Cummings, courtesy of chanceprojects

of middle-class values which fits this new world like a glove, encompassing those parts of Britain which seem to be closest to the Californian ideal of a knowledge economy dependent on entrepreneurship, creativity, pursuit of the good life, and the like. It is to be found in places like parts of Cambridge, the outskirts of London, the City of London, and so on.

There are a number of reasons why so much attention is focused on the new professional strata. To begin with, middling-class people like managers and professionals have the power to define what counts as a good job and this inevitably favours their skills. Moreover, it is they – as analysts, academics, journalists and pundits – who get to describe to the rest of the population the changes that are taking place. So, for example, home working by working-class women is a peripheral issue, but home working by middle-class men and women is a matter of national angst.

Clearly, this is a world which is internationally connected to similar enclaves elsewhere. It is a world that turns on 'global' connection – or, more accurately, connecting to those parts of the globe that are like it. But, equally clearly, it *does not speak for all of all British cities, but rather for small parts of just some of those cities.* Let's take just one example: the information technology industry. The UK is estimated to be short of between 50,000 and 70,000 information technology specialists, for which about half of the jobs are located in London (Local Futures

Group, 1999). The information technology industry is highly geographically concentrated; 46% of the total UK information technology workforce is in London and the South East (with 18% in London alone), with only small amounts of the workforce to be found in each other region. In class terms, these concentrations are even greater: 55% of UK managerial and professional jobs are in London and the South East. We might well ask where the rest of the population is in all this. One part of the answer is that the 'new knowledge/service economy' produces its own proletariat – in call centres, on assembly lines for producing high-tech products, and to service the continuing need for cleaners, security guards, waitresses and waiters. There is then something of a dualism built in to the high-tech knowledge economy itself.

But it would be wrong to reduce the social structure to a simplistic dichotomy between the new professionals on the one hand and a stratum of low-paid service providers on the other. (This would be to reproduce the new/old antagonistic dichotomisation on which so much of Blairite thinking depends – except in this case the poor are just as much a part of the new as are the rich.) As well as these groups there are those which work in and around the burgeoning cultural and media industries, defined in the widest of senses. Energetic, enterprising, often rich in cultural capital but often working for low pay as they struggle from one project to another (McRobbie, 1999). Then there are the bodies of public sector and care workers (in transport, in councils, in health, in education) without whom cities could not function at all. And there are great numbers of people employed in a wide variety of manufacturing and service industries which do not form part of the classic Blairite image of the new economy. Most working-class people with jobs work in one of five types of job: as members of the clerical workforce, as members of the sales force, in construction or as drivers or as machine operators. We need urban economic policies which address the full range of these skills and occupations.

At its extreme, then, the Blairite vision of the economy is insufficiently recognising of diversity to be an adequate basis for policy. We need an economic policy – and an urban realm more generally – which is genuinely for the many not for the few. And cities? They are diverse. Yet in economic policy terms nearly all appear to be following the same 'new economy' agenda. What are the industries cities should attract? Why, finance, media and information technology (plus biotechnology if someone could make a profit from it). How should cities be set up? So that they will attract workers in these industries –

especially younger managers and professionals who will give a city the buzz. In turn, working-class people will find a niche – servicing these middle-class people, acting as evidence of multicultural cosmopolitanism or exemplifying problem communities. What they will not be is central to urban regeneration. They will only be allowed to cheer from the sidelines as the niceness squeeze of this gentrification continues.

This is perhaps why, in the end, the brief for the Rogers Report had so little to ask or say about jobs and employment. Because that would be to open up the question of who urban regeneration is actually for. And yet there is a sustained demand for jobs that working-class people could fill. Indeed, in many cities the problem is the lack of enough of these kinds of jobs (Turok and Edge, 1999). Repeated claims over the gains in professional and managerial jobs and the declines in junior non-manual, and skilled, semi-skilled and unskilled manual jobs need to be set in context.

So, what must be addressed is the inherent inequality of so much of what is on offer (the very nature of the 'economic growth' strategy itself) and the increase in inequality to which it is in danger of leading. And in preparing to do this, we need to be clear that we are not having to fight against inevitable counterforces: there is no shortage of things that can be done. The language of 'the gentrification of the economy' allows us not to have to think about the needs of the majority of the population.

The other urban economy

So, is it true that a new global knowledge economy is inevitable and the only course of action for cities is to go with the flow? We don't think so. We believe that this is an extraordinarily selective view of the nature of both the global economy and cities.

First of all, we would want to point to what counts as the urban economy. What is missing from so many new urban accounts is any sense of the extraordinary diversity of urban economies. It is as if much of city life passes these accounts by. It is a strange land fit only for strangers. Take, for example, the case of the proliferation of 'trade-it' magazines which show the constant hum of a wealth of undocumented exchange. Or take those car scrap yards which are witness to the constant recycling of so much of what is produced in cities. Or take the cars and vans of salespersons and repairers which represent a growing mobile workforce, constantly on the move and keeping in touch with base by mobile phone and computer. This invisibility needs to be brought to the surface of our perception, and valued.

Then there is what counts as knowledge. Cities are rich soups of knowledge of all kinds, not just the cognitive-technical knowledge which seems to be at the centre of so much of the new economy. We believe that it is necessary to expand our idea of what counts as knowledge so that it has much more diverse and creative connotations which reflect the diversity and creativity of cities and their inhabitants. The idea of a knowledge-based economy can be extended far beyond high technology or the media or finance to include a rich ecology of skills, such as the knowledge of those involved in the hotel and restaurant trades, transport and communication, much of the public sector and catering and cleaning. In particular, there is the knowledge involved in actually educating people, in interpersonal service delivery, in caring industries like the public services, and the aesthetic dimensions of design activities from engineering and furniture – moving through to the arts and crafts. Of course, these activities are rarely thought of as particularly dynamic or cutting-edge but they can be understood in a quite different light when they all come together in the economic intensity of cities; in a sense they *are* the knowledge economy for most cities.

These different forms of knowledge – so everyday that we tend to forget about them in grand new visions of the future – make up the everyday urban economy. A cursory glance at the Yellow Pages of any British city – in the North or the South – will confirm this, as we meander through an array of personal, professional, and commercial services, light industry and small firms of one sort or another, second-hand and recycling trades, recreation and leisure activities, transport and distribution trades, and so on. These are the enduring activities of cities defined as an internal economy, drawing opportunity from the sheer density of population within them. Their presence allows us to see the economics of cities in terms of *demand-led growth* in an internal market that meets the needs of its residents and visitors, that provides scale opportunities for firms to expand and, perhaps, trade nationally and internationally, that expands and diversifies as a consequence of the presence of other trades (eg spin-off from existing firms, subcontracting, specialised or associated trades), and that sustains a large recycling industry of second-hand or modified goods.

And there is more to the urban economy than the highly diversified private sector. Care workers at home and beyond, in the welfare sector and the public services too, are also a mainstay of the urban economy. Without them, the formal economy suffers huge costs of reproduction related to traffic congestion, poor education, ill-health, inadequate childcare, and so on. Then, many of these activities are sectors of welfare expenditure and, as such, generators of further demand. Further, their dense infrastructure and weight of expertise (for example hospitals and their staff) constitute an enormous urban investment, that is, sunk capital for intergenerational economic activity. Indeed, this is exactly how we might also wish to think of the vast reservoir of unpaid labour in homes as well as the services offered in the third sector by non-profit organisations. Both are vital resources upon which the economy of paid activity draws continuously for its various 'service needs' or to off-set its costs. All this wider range of economic (and 'non-economic') activity needs fuller recognition in urban policy, both in its own right (and the conditions which might enable its better functioning) and in its relations to the more often acknowledged parts of the urban system.

This is *another kind of knowledge economy*, one that mobilises knowledge of how to make people feel valued, knowledge of how to value experience, knowledge of how to interact with people. These are the different kinds of knowledge that the private sector service industries are themselves constantly striving to mobilise. The irony is that they are here on their door step in profusion. There is, in other words, much more to what counts as urban prosperity than securing international competitiveness in the global knowledge economy through corporate means and, in planning the city, we need to acknowledge the existence, skills and requirements of all urban residents.

So, as we sign up to the new global knowledge economy we are also signing up to a very particular and unequal kind of growth. It is one which fails to recognise so many of the qualities of city populations, reducing them to that which produces competitive edge. It is one which often only recognises a few industries as key, neglecting other industries which are just as economically important. It is one which fails to recognise the complexity of cities as a reservoir of interactions which is one of the reasons why cities are so innovative. It is one which fails to recognise the still pivotal role of much of the public sector. And it is one which has no means of valuing the role of non-paid work or the third sector, except as sponsorship opportunities. And, to make things worse, it is a form of growth which is based on concentrating economic activity in a few congested and steamed-up parts of Britain while neglecting everywhere else and on intensifying the knowledge capacity of a few very particular places (and indeed adding to these by allowing yet more similarly knowledgeable talent to arrive from outside the country) in a way which at the same time short-circuits growth everywhere else. In truth, national economic growth therefore means making sure that growth is a racing certainty in the 'fertile crescent' of London and the South East, and parts of the South West and East Anglia, with a side-bet that growth will foray out into the rest of the country in times of boom.

Choices for urban economic policy

Luckily for us, we live in a time when economic choices still exist as it is realised (by those not overwhelmed by the knowledge economy) that no one root form of the market or capitalism exists (Coates, 2000). The experience of Eastern Europe and the former Soviet states has shown that establishing a market involves an extraordinary tracery of institutions, histories and cultures – corporate forms, legal frameworks, relationships of trust, and so on – which will vary widely from place to place. The experience of capitalism in various parts of the world has shown that it takes on many forms – there are, literally, many capitalisms, from the spun-sugar networks of trade and finance built up by the overseas Chinese, to the heavily institutionalised capitalism of Germany, from the Darwinian struggle to innovate found in Silicon Valley to the cultural tramlines of Japan. Then, we have seen a gradual realisation that many forms of economic organisation can and do thrive under capitalism, large, small, hierarchical, networked, directed, cooperative, family-owned, shareholder-owned, and so on. There is a kind of capitalist ecology.

There are choices available for economic policy, including at the urban level. Indeed, in all likelihood, the more diverse this ecology the better since economies which are diverse have more ability to adapt and innovate over the long term. Let us look at some of the available choices, some of which can be made to work to egalitarian ends:

▶ *Harnessing best practice from big corporations:* cities and nations all over the world have become obsessed with attracting mobile investment and will do almost anything to meet their needs, from offering huge subsidies to removing perceived barriers to profitability. This is in stark contrast to increasing support among at least some big capitalist firms for social objectives which reach beyond mere maximisation of shareholder value. This opportunity could be used to negotiate investment in local public goods from investors as well as to press for higher local expectations both in the workplace and in the use of local resources – facilitated perhaps through revisions to company law to recognise stakeholder interests. Policy makers should note, for example, the increasing number of studies, since at least the 1940s, which show that democracy in the workplace is not only good for workers but can have positive effects on profits.

▶ *Business support programmes to spread the economic portfolio of a city:* current policy, especially in deprived areas, focuses on encouraging entrepreneurship and business start-ups, while emerging policy promises support for (knowledge-based) clusters. What, however, about the myriad of existing firms of different size and sectoral variety that make up our cities, and which also require a supportive urban fabric that allows them to reduce transaction costs and maximise opportunity? Part of the challenge lies in providing easy access to local business services, pooled resources, and partnerships with other firms to allow specialisation and reciprocity. But it also lies in generic upgrading of the supply-side infrastructure. This clearly includes investment in the knowledge infrastructure for high-tech innovation and that for formal education, but it also includes the learning that goes on in sites of practised craft, manual, distributive, professional and caring skills. It also requires sustained support for the public and welfare services to secure a constant stream of future competences and capabilities.

▶ *Policies to stimulate and sustain demand in the urban economy:* normally, demand is managed by the central government through its control over the terms of credit, taxation, and direct public expenditure. And here, the government's slow moves towards redistributing income and its signals to improve financial access for low-income groups are welcome not only on grounds of social justice, but also as a way of stimulating expenditure. A degree of fiscal freedom at the urban level, however, would give city authorities greater leverage to stimulate local demand through public programmes of various sorts (eg housing, parks, festivals, transport) and simultaneously meet local welfare and consumer needs. Short of this, local authorities need to consider the implications of seeing cities as gigantic markets for new and recycled goods and services, which might then force attention on the economics of supplying facilities for recycling, outlets for second-hand goods, and spaces for markets in general.

▶ This leads on to the pivotal role of *environmental thinking*, which sees cities as globally interconnected ecologies and which has been responsible for important new urban initiatives; like recycling, new forms of packaging, farmers' markets, fairly traded goods, and the refurbishing of telephones and computers for developing countries. These too are economically worthwhile activities.

▶ *Recognition for the increasing centrality of the social/civic economy*, centred around not-for-profit activities and affordable trade. Our age of jobless growth has seen the rise of new forms of transaction supporting poorer people in cities, from community banks to LETS and time dollars schemes. It has also seen the expansion of third sector organisations training and employing excluded groups to provide vital social services not covered by the market or the state (eg recycled furniture for low-income groups, childcare schemes in poor neighbourhoods, maintenance of housing estates). The government – through its urban and neighbourhood regeneration policies masterminded by the Social Exclusion Unit and the DETR – has shown itself to be genuinely supportive of third sector initiatives and community enterprises, but generally in the context of markedly deprived areas, and as a stepping stone back into the formal economy. We would argue the case for strengthening the social economy as an alternative to the formal economy concerned with meeting social needs and capacity building, and we see no need to restrict experimentation to particular types of urban area.

In short, there are real economic choices that can and are being made about the future of cities. There seems to be no necessary preference for any one form of economic governance of cities over another, and a convincing argument can be made for diversity of governance as an economic strength. In turn, this implies a role for the state as the means of ensuring that maximum experimentation continues, the guarantor of wider economic participation, innovation and choice.

In the rest of Europe, a greater recognition of these arguments has produced all kinds of experiments that we could usefully take note of. Of these experiments, perhaps the most exciting have been those to do with the organisation of time, in the attempt to produce the city anew by placing it not just in space but also in time (eg spaces for contemplation – see Chapters 4 and 5). These initiatives address one of the great taboos of our age, the need to make room for free time. The truly democratic city must not blindly endorse the urban economy characterised by all-hours, speed and utilitarian achievement. It should also protect the right to be free of the demands of productive labour and material pursuit. Increasingly, the pressure on those in work (paid and unpaid) is to work longer hours and to raise productivity to the point of early burnout, while the pressure on those not in work (both voluntary and forced) is to be reintegrated into economic activity, for this is seen as the principal source of social identity and recognition.

The 'thin' cities of the global knowledge economy, cities whose only purpose often seems to be to speed the commodity on its way, must be made liveable by acknowledging just how complex cities are and how, in turn, that complexity provides spaces and times of experimentation, spaces and times of free play which by providing breaks in the helter-skelter of consumption add enormous richness to the texture of urban life.

If this is the case, then what we need to design, rather more than we need designer waterfronts and an infinity of coffee houses and sandwich bars, are cities for all the people, cities in which those who want work can find it and, increasingly, find work that fits their talents, dreams and perspicacities. And, as we saw in Chapter 1, one version of that dream is to be found in government report after government report. Yet, here we are, at the beginning of a new millennium, all but blinded by the gleam of a knowledge economy which, ironically, does not seem to know how to do it. We think that cities for all the people are

© Neil Cummings, courtesy of chanceprojects

possible and that what really prevents their birth is often more to do with the attitudes of the guardians of the knowledge economy who are willing to put up with the downside of the maldistribution of resources just so long as their own position is protected. Of course, these guardians *care* – after all, that's what we do nowadays – but they care only as long as it does not threaten the number of good restaurants. Marx and Engels put it rather well:

> A part of the bourgeoisie is desirous of redressing social grievances, in order to secure the continued existence of bourgeois society. To this section belong economists, philanthropists, humanitarians, improvers of the conditions of the working class, organisers of charity, members of society for the protection of animals, temperance fanatics, hole-and-corner reformers of every possible kind.... Free Trade: for the benefit of the working class. Protective duties: for the benefit of the working class. Prison Reform: for the benefit of the working class ... the bourgeois is a bourgeois – for the benefit of the working class. (Marx and Engels, 1968, pp 58-9)

Famously, Marx and Engels went on to diagnose many of the problems of scabrous industrial cities and rotting working-class rookeries as being the result of the nature of the ownership of the economy. A great deal has clearly changed since the 19th century but, as we step over the brink into the 21st century, certain things have not changed nearly as much as they should. And, until they do, our cities will still speak the language of exclusion, still paint landscapes of despair, still taste of bitter fruit.

We believe that the chief problem for our cities is not some 'inevitable' global economy, it is not lack of new forms of corporate organisation, it is not lack of enthusiasm for new working practices and it is not absence of clustering. The problem is lack of political will and above all the lack of willingness to extend to the economies of cities the same democratic rights that could be found in their political systems. Why do we need to think of capitalism and the market as remorseless, inevitable forces in our lives – not to be disrupted – when the rest of our lives are increasingly constructed as choices? Only because we are willing to cede them this mastery.

4

Rights to the city

The recovery of this mastery might begin with questions concerning who decides about what we want from our cities – in the nature of urban democracy. The creativity and prosperity of cities is as dependent on the opportunity they provide for social expression and public participation as on the quality of their social and economic assets. But cities present particular challenges to democracy. If we think of cities not in terms of their physicality or built design only, but also in terms of constellations of lives, then the intensity with which those lives are lived, together with the diversity of lives which are brought together, present both special problems and particular opportunities. Our argument is that in a globalised world democracy faces challenges everywhere, in cities and outside them, but in cities one comes face to face with perhaps the most acute expressions of these challenges. Much of the argument below, therefore, concerns the nature of a healthy democracy in general, but it has been provoked by our thinking about cities and it is, perhaps, in cities that such a democracy will face its severest test.

What we are searching for here is, firstly, an approach which might enable participation and debate (and even disagreement) in a way which recognises the rich diversity of cities and the conflicting claims as well as creative tensions which that throws up. But, secondly, we believe it important to establish also some notion of shared belonging, a sense of common citizenship, an idea that there might after all be such a thing as society. A city politics which could achieve this would be – what we are aiming at – a confident democracy based on active citizenship, even when it clashes with 'official' visions of what is right and who has a right.

New Labour too is interested in democratisation, but we wonder if in the same way. Our interest lies in the promotion of an egalitarian society through social empowerment and respect for diversity. The government seems to be more interested in delivery mechanisms and the efficiency of different institutional options (eg the balance of responsibilities between central government, local government, and community organisations). This is evident in its plans to modernise local government, but also across the large number of pilot programmes with an urban remit that have been launched after 1997 – New Deal for Communities, Social Inclusion Partnerships (in Scotland), Employment Zones, Education Action Zones, Sure Start, Excellence in Cities, and so on. Across these programmes can be traced an underlying concern with what is best delivered through central government initiatives and what through neighbourhood or community organisations (with local government frequently side-lined). As for the purpose of democratisation, the prime interest – rather like during war-time – seems to lie in getting people to pull together in blighted communities around an agenda prescribed by the government, often with a strong dose of commentary on the virtues of community and moral obligation. This we find in the policies harnessing Welfare to Work, in declarations about the virtues of 'civic patriotism' based on voluntary participation and corporate donations, and in the National Strategy for Neighbourhood Renewal, with its army of social entrepreneurs, neighbourhood wardens and community leaders. We applaud the call for active citizenship in all this, but do wonder whether (moral) prescription is the way forward.

The Rogers Report has a refreshingly less prescriptive tone, as is evident from its support for public consultation in urban design and grass-roots proposals in Urban Priority Areas. Rogers also recognises the relationship between the city's open spaces and the non-instrumental gains associated with public access to these spaces. He is keen to reclaim streets, parks and squares as

> ... somewhere to relax and enjoy the urban experience, a venue for a range of different activities, from outdoor eating to street entertainment; from sport and play areas to a venue for civic or political functions; and most importantly of all as a place for walking and sitting-out. (Urban Task Force, 1999a, p 57)

This interpretation of urban democracy follows a long line of theorisation of public spaces as a source of citizenship, sparked by relaxation, and mingling with strangers and friends. We have no quibble with the case for pleasant open spaces made accessible to all. But we would question any automatic linkage of public spaces with civility on the grounds that such spaces are increasingly sites for private enjoyment and retreat rather than socialisation with strangers.

Right to participate

If we are in search of the public realm, we need to look beyond the public spaces of the city, starting with the public services and welfare services, which took a battering under the Tories. Libraries, museums, health, housing, transport, education, and the other welfare services – if generously funded, professionally delivered, and universally provided – will meet basic needs and provide a minimum set of opportunities for social citizenship (in this regard we welcome the tone of the Spring 2000 budget). Although urban projects centred around these services lack the sound-bite of great architectural projects, the truth is that many urban problems such as homelessness, crime, social inequality, entrapment, resentment and despair at the bottom of society can be linked to the erosion of opportunities provided by the welfare state. Why do we continue to marvel at the army of homeless people, rebellious youths, disillusioned unemployed people, desperate single parents, dejected pensioners, when it is so clear that their expectation of a fair and equitable society has been shattered? The real malaise relates to the loss of opportunity felt by so many people to become something in society. Why then not place welfare upgrading at the centre of a new urban policy? The civic city cannot be the city of constrained welfare.

The government might respond that it is precisely these sorts of questions which lie behind its current efforts to secure convergence between its welfare and urban policies. A number of departments have introduced welfare policies with an area-based focus. We have Health Action Zones, Education Action Zones, Sure Start, New Start, the Burglary Initiative, Early Excellence Centres, Healthy Schools, Renewal Areas, and so on. These, together with urban initiatives such as the Single Regeneration Budget and New Deal for Communities, do indeed focus on the social, welfare and employment needs of the country's most deprived urban areas.

Our worry, however, is that *spatial* targeting of this kind might legitimate the substitution of universal welfare by focusing support in particularly hard-hit localities or vulnerable groups. This would not come as a surprise given the scale of unmet need and capacity erosion after the years of welfare neglect by the last government. But it would be a shift towards ghettoising particular areas and social groups as the sinks of society for which 'special help' is needed. It might end up restricting access to state welfare for the mainstream – spatial and social – thereby challenging *the principle of universal provision of a bundle of basic welfare rights that all individuals carry with them*, regardless of where they are and their particular socio-economic circumstances at a given moment in time. Any such shift raises fundamental questions not only about who is 'deserving', but, as we argue below, also about democracy itself through the erosion of universal access to the basic resources for self-development and expression.

The civic city has to be one which enhances social justice *for all*, serving to meet needs and unlock human potential. This requires intervention at the national level, in addition, of course, to actions through urban policy. The restoration of universal welfare is a step in the right direction, as is the offer of the economic opportunities we outlined in Chapter 3. There are also other steps, two of which are particularly important for developing active citizenship: building capabilities and socialisation.

Capabilities

The economist Amartya Sen (1992) has proposed that in the long run only actions designed to develop human capabilities will help to tackle social inequality. There seems to be a broad consensus – and we agree – that education and learning are one core capability. Governments around the world recognise this, but only too often, as we see in Blunkett's Britain, they reduce education to immediate labour market needs. Our point is that a society that values the developmental power of education should provide ample scope for learning on intrinsic grounds, as a non-utilitarian good. Education in this sense contributes to the fulfilment of human potential as well as constituting a pre-condition for democratic participation.

So education has to include more than the provision of free or affordable access to schools and higher educational opportunities, although we do not undervalue the importance of providing well-funded institutions of a manageable size run by competent professionals. It has to provide more than on-the-job and off-the-job training. It has to enshrine the right to take leave from work or domestic duties – perhaps through paid sabbaticals – for educational improvement and training. The government's current plans for lifelong education are a step in the right direction, but the coupling with short-term labour market outcomes needs to be loosened to include access as a means of self-empowerment and capability-building. In 1992, for example, the Danes experimented with a voluntary Paid Leave Scheme which released employees in the public sector for a year to pursue activities with no strings attached, while their jobs were offered to unemployed persons as an opportunity for work experience. The original guiding principle of universal education needs to be recovered through state support for a variety of centres of learning available to different generations and communities. For example, 'folk universities' (as they are called in Sweden) might be actively promoted and funded by municipal authorities across a city's neighbourhoods, offering courses in the humanities, arts and sciences to people of all ages. Similarly, support might be given to the multitude of voluntary and non-profit organisations surviving on a shoestring to provide courses of different sorts, from access to information technology to wool-spinning and adult literacy.

Inevitably, the critics will ask how these proposals should be funded. The above ideas require sustained provision, which explains the unease of governments worried about raising taxes to fund high quality welfare. There are, however, radical alternatives which are worth exploring. One is the possibility of a *lifelong social endowment account* for all citizens. The political visionary Roberto Unger (1998) argues that, for reasons of affordability, the national pool of funds could be linked to the economy's productivity and growth performance over a given period of calculation. The account would provide for lifetime education, rather than give individuals free choice over expenditure (in order to avoid rash decisions at an early age to splash out on an expensive luxury item). Unger suggests that it could discriminate in favour of those most at a disadvantage, by including a fixed and a variable part, with the latter part increasing "by one measure according to a principle of compensation for special need, for physical, social, or cognitive disadvantage" (p 267). The account could even include non-cash options such as public service as payment for training received, so as to ease financial pressure and target usage of the account (eg Singapore runs a bond scheme that provides foreign education in return for 10 years work in the civil service). In short, the building of capabilities – through lifelong education in this example – does not have to depend on extravagant tax hikes which will be rejected by the electorate.

A civilised society should wish to build capabilities as a democratic right. And, indeed, cities are full of the bustle of learning in under-recognised initiatives such as universities of the third age, people attending night schools, budding musicians and artists gathering in damp venues, volunteers keen to learn first aid and counselling, courses to develop practical expertise in the martial arts, cooking, outdoor pursuits, and so on. In fact, one of the roles of cities is to provide meeting places for such activities which are the very essence of a confident democracy. It would be nice to think that the government's proposed urban academies and plans to run community centres through schools in poor areas could be expanded to all areas and broadened to include these learning ventures.

Socialisation

Any recovery of the commons in our cities surely has to recognise the value of solidarity. This, in turn, highlights the problem of socialisation into forms of citizenship based on solidarity. We focus below on three possible sources:

► A knowledgeable and discursive *political community*. At the end of the 19th century, a prime deficit was the availability of information as a public good, and real-time communication. Into the 21st century, there is no shortage of instantaneous access to news and views around the world. Proximity and visibility in public spaces are not the only means for public engagement and the culture of acting out in public has become all pervasive. Thus we do not think it pragmatic or realistic to return to the great debating halls or gatherings in public squares or community educational centres of the past as the prime instruments of politicisation and political learning. It is the principle of political engagement that is worth retaining, supported through a number of urban institutions. Schools could have a primary role to play, through debate over issues of interest to students. John Prescott's enthusiasm for a Children's Parliament could be extended to every school in Britain. This, to us, seems more effective than lecturing students on civics and citizenship, by mobilising political engagement in innovative ways and through everyday issues. There is no reason why this principle cannot be pursued in after-school centres, workplaces and other places of daytime and evening gathering (eg evening courses, clubs, etc). There is also considerable scope for the creative use of media-based debate. The spectacular success of televised chat shows is testimony, drawing as it does on mass revelation. We are not necessarily defending the material and manner of chat shows, which often dramatise and degrade acutely personal problems, but rather their potential to expose, discuss and change opinion over especially sensitive social and ethical matters (eg family violence, incest, sexual practices). Further, the mounting success of citizens' juries to deliberate over public issues confirms the still healthy public desire for political engagement. Some of this engagement is now occurring at a distance through the Internet, and not only for semi-legal and minority political groups scanning the globe for support. In cities such as Amsterdam, Bologna and Athens, the facilitation of Internet access to the public by the city administrations has also encouraged public debate (albeit circumscribed) about local services, planning and political issues (Tsagarousianou et al, 1998).

▶ Combining politics and pleasure through *sociability*. Citizenship is nurtured through social contact in places you can return to and value as meeting places. We need to rediscover the forgotten role of everyday institutions such as public libraries and community centres, as centres of light sociability through shared experience. Building on the idea of using schools for mixed purposes, why not have social centres in every urban neighbourhood, governed from below, with no pressure to attend or undertake prescribed activities, offering recreation, leisure, and meeting rooms. As Sam Fleischacker (1998) argues, these 'insignificant' or 'particle' community centres should not seek to politicise, but work on the value of political education through sociability. A strong example is provided by the movements of 1968 – from worker and feminist struggles to student protests – which managed to combine theory, political action and enjoyment in quite staggering ways. They were as much about political critique and struggle as they were about alternative life-styles and values, drawing on a social energy that gave life to festivals, parades, communes, and many other solidaristic pleasures and experiments. The social energy breathed life back into political activity, and most importantly, became a source of radical opening of new and sustainable possibilities and projects. It is this kind of hedonism without consumerism (Soper, 1998) that we need to recover as the driving force of a new politics of transformation.

▶ Our interest in pleasure is not gratuitous, or put differently, not a prioritisation of individual rights over social obligations. The problem of how to inculcate *civic values* does need tackling, and in ways which draw in everybody. Neither of the above two socialisation strategies work for those averse to social and civic engagement. But, corrective action based on indignation (eg punishment, exclusion) and other similar responses should be a last resort, deployed against the threat of violence to others. To encourage citizenship as an everyday practice, people need experience of negotiating diversity and adversity. Yet this is exactly what has been put to the test in our times of associating with only those like you or whom you like. Citizenship has to develop though *practice,* and by taking individuals out of their daily communities. One possibility is to encourage citizens – through the offer of incentives (eg income or worthwhile training certification) – to undertake social and civic duties of various sorts through state and voluntary organisations for a given period in early adulthood. The government's plans to encourage 16-24-year-olds to undertake up to 200 hours of voluntary work or employees to take a take a day off work for voluntary work is a very small step in the right direction. There are, however, other successful experiments in US cities based on longer commitments and better rewards (Dahle, 1999). One scheme – City Year – tells the story of participation – motivated by a modest living allowance and partial college scholarships – of young adults from all walks of life on community projects such as cleaning up vacant lots, providing HIV education, tutoring other students, and helping elderly people. Another successful scheme – Public Allies – promotes citizenship by placing young people in 10-month paid apprenticeships with local non-profit organisations.

In summary, rights to the city must offer individuals the possibility of becoming something/someone else through access to the means for developing capabilities, political judgement and sociability. Without these rights we are left with only the traditional politics of prescription and elite designation. This is a politics without the creativity and innovation that flows from social empowerment and participation. And, as it happens, cities are replete with such energy, as we can see from the undiminished involvement of people in collective projects of one sort or another, from schoolchildren visiting old people's homes, voluntary groups coming together in environmental projects, and direct participation in popular campaigns such as those around road building programmes.

City politics

Some of our proposals deliberately transcend the urban scale, as universals in social scope and geography. How do they relate to the city of difference and mixture we outlined in Chapter 2, as well as to our claims concerning the contested and plural nature of politics today? How do they relate to civility and citizenship in *cities*?

What we have in mind is a *transversal politics* (Yuval-Davis, 1999) with two distinctive ends. Such a politics seeks, first, to reconcile universal goals with particular interests by forging solidarities across the disparate sites and social demands of the heterogeneous contemporary city: hence our emphasis on the commons and in ways which have nothing to do with consensus over goals. Second, it seeks to provide mechanisms for airing differences and, as far as possible, a level playing field for contestation. Power differentials and inequality run through the fabric of cities, thus it would be naïve to think that conflict can be eliminated or resolved in favour of all citizens. However, universals such as the right to work, welfare and capable citizenship can be seen as essential resources for social participation and empowerment, helping not only to alleviate some of the causes of intolerance and violence towards others, but also to build voice and capacity for opposition across the social spectrum.

Cities necessitate and can also contribute to a transversal politics. One of the characteristics which we highlighted in Chapter 2 was the fact of cities as spatial phenomena. Spatiality is crucially important to the quality of life and we believe it could, fully recognised, be a significant component in forging a progressive city politics. There is no end to possibility here. Let us look at some options:

▶ Part of the essential character of cities is their *geographical density*. As we have said, this can be both exhilarating and unbearable (and often both on the same day). We need to imagine the physical geography of cities with this in mind, understanding what 'moods' different physical places can encourage, and planning for there to be a mixture of paces and places. High streets and local centres can be foci of the intensity, with a mix of uses designed to bring people together. But there need also to be breathing spaces – and Rogers is right to emphasise this – places where people can have the space (just as earlier we spoke of the time) to abstract themselves from the rush and tumble, to slow down. Such places may be small parks, or libraries, or (free) local galleries, or just a clump of trees with a bench or two, perhaps even wasteland and railway sidings. But they are necessary to the city's survivability – and they should be found throughout the city, not only in the areas of the well-to-do. And slowing down is as much about recovery as it is about urban reflectivity and creativity in the city of economic diversity, as we saw in Chapter 3.

▶ To balance notions of the city as the pulse for global economic competitiveness, we need to think of cities as *stopping places*, and not just for the workers of the global knowledge economy. A housing policy geared towards the latter and long-term residents alone seems a narrow response to the role of cities as places to which itinerants, migrants, tourists, escapees and opportunity-seekers gravitate. Brownfield reconversion, if we want to call it that, should be also about imaginative schemes to shelter, feed, and encourage itinerants who seek such support. If we increasingly accept that cities are places of passing through, we need to reject the culture of fear and loathing towards asylum seekers, other migrants, the homeless and the visibly unemployed. Why do we seem so happy to see other migrants such as business people and celebrities stay at the Dorchester? And we should not need to justify positive action purely on commercial terms, as implied by Stephen O'Brien, the chief executive of London First, who suggests we

… cannot have a commercially successful city if you have a lot of people sitting on the outside, because eventually they will start throwing bricks. And, across a wide range of fronts, business leadership and involvement is integral to creating and sustaining a successful city. (*Financial Times*, 2 December, 1999, p 8)

The action needs defending on welfare grounds. No civilised city can live comfortably with the knowledge that the incidence of illness and accident and the mortality rate among the homeless is much higher than among the middle-income groups.

▶ We must learn, when 'planning the city', really to *think spatially*, with all the complexities that involves. A public park may serve as an example in microcosm: how can it be enabled to be used by children, dog owners, frail and elderly people and those who just want to play football? We need to learn about the kinds of social power (which may be no more, and no more malicious in intent, than the danger of a flying football) which enable one group to claim space at the expense of others; and then we need to build a city space which can cope with such conflicts. This might include creating protected spaces such as Coram's Field – a park in central London created in 1936, to enable children to play freely and in safety. Public parks really *are* only a microcosm, however, of the wider array of differential powers which construct the social geography of the city as a whole. There is a vast difference between the estates on which people are trapped by poverty, and into which outsiders rarely venture, and the gated communities of the rich, designed to keep others out. It is this power-filled social geography which we must address. At present British cities do not suffer from, for instance, the degree of class and ethnic segregation which scars the cities of the USA (one reason why spatial targeting, for instance, of poverty programmes, is inappropriate here). We must beware of tendencies in that direction. If groups feel themselves to be excluded or poorly serviced there may result a movement to 'set up on their own' in exasperation. We must ask ourselves if we want our cities to become mosaics of geographically inward-looking communities. As we said in Chapter 2 the broader tendencies are to pull apart the isomorphism of community and place and to emphasise the multiplicity of all our identities. We must work towards an urban social geography which can allow those tendencies too to flourish.

▶ Again, as we said in Chapter 2, we need an explicit social policy of mobility and access. Cities which are as unfriendly as ours currently are to the ageing and the frail are simply not humane cities. The GLC was maligned for encouraging pavement ramps – but now they are everywhere. And many 'mobility' policies will be as small – and yet as significant – as this. Uneven pavements can be a nightmare for many to negotiate. One of the early initiatives of women's committees, for instance, was simply to improve street lighting in particularly threatening stretches of road. The lack of such lights *creates* disadvantage. But a social policy of mobility is not for the disadvantaged alone in the progressive city. Affordable transport, ease of mobility and access to communications has become a priority issue for the majority of the urban population in our age of global mobility and communication. In response, many cities around the world are now seeking to provide cheap but effective public transportation as well as free access to the Internet (eg Bologna).

▶ Similarly, we need to recognise the role of cities as places of socialisation and sociability beyond riverside cafes, shopping mall atria and bijou restaurants. An urban cultural policy should acknowledge and encourage the vast network of everyday associations of sociability which already exists across all parts of the city. A very substantial number of visits into and across cities are about meeting friends, attending youth and adult recreation or education clubs of one sort or another, renewing community links, be they religious, ethnic, gendered or otherwise. British cities are replete with associations – from pottery groups and amateur theatre groups to scout clubs and swimming clubs – which are the very essence of learning, organisational capability, and civic participation. There really *is* a lot going on in our cities beyond the life of firms and work, melancholy and alienation, state and other institutions of governance. It is simply not true that we no longer participate in society. Everyday participation needs to be recognised as important for urban life, not only through the provision of resources and premises as is the habit in Scandinavian countries, but also by facilitating visibility through festivals, floats, street-events, parades, craft fairs and so on. This too can be part of a confident democracy.

▶ We need to recognise spaces of democracy that lie beyond the democratic state and representative politics. The density of cities is also the density of institutions which represent diverse communities of interest. These include business organisations and interest groups, family organisations, voluntary groups and religious organisations, lobbying groups and protest campaigns, and so on. Cities are massive reservoirs of institutionalised activity, around which urban democracy can be built and extended. This could take place through public scrutiny of local government plans through public hearings and electronic town hall meetings; consultative and participatory decision making within government, businesses and other governance institutions; inclusion of stakeholders in planning decisions as well as the voice of less experienced stakeholders (Healey, 1997; Sandercock, 1998); city plans produced by grass-roots organisations and local communities, as in Porto Allegre in Brazil, even if this means placing restrictions on the powerful (eg taxes on pollution, type of inward investment, working conditions); schemes such as derelict land reclamation by community groups, recreation plans drawn up by school children, and control of neighbourhood regeneration budgets by communities themselves. These are all ideas based on real experiments with urban democratisation around the world.

© Neil Cummings, courtesy of chanceprojects

5

Afterword

There are many urban policy options that can counterbalance the familiar recommendations from national and city leaders to redesign British cities, promote urban competitiveness, and deliver efficient governance. The central question, however, is less about the range of policy options available, and more about what we want from our cities and how best to achieve the desired goals. Surprisingly, there has been hardly any public debate on what cities are for and who should decide on their futures. The purpose of this document has been to spark this debate, by staking out an alternative vision of urban life centred around the energies of its inhabitants and geared towards meeting social needs and developing capabilities. We have argued for recognition of the everyday economy of cities involved with providing jobs and services to meet local demand and local needs, and we have argued for placing confidence in the powers of active citizenship and experiments in urban democracy.

If cities are unique sites of intense social interaction and juxtaposed difference, as we have argued, then the effects of spatial intensity and diversity on their quality of life and their economic performance do need to be taken seriously. The Rogers Report is clearly sensitive to these issues, in pressing for an holistic and sustainable urban experience, good quality design and architecture, compact sites, and pleasant open spaces. Its acknowledgement of the spatiality of the city is to be welcomed. But this spatiality is also about dealing with the effects of diverse communities and interests living together in close proximity, This is why we have stressed the rights of being, becoming and interconnecting in the city; rights which do not flow alone from the ways in which physical space is organised, but also from the developmental and expressive opportunities given to people. But, as such, our interest has been less in the search for a common good or consensus – an impossible challenge in the heterogeneous city – than in ways in which living together in cities is an enriching and creative experience.

In our vision, the temporality of the city – its rhythm and pace – has also been a crucial factor. Richard Sennett (1998), among others, is right to warn of the dangers of a new 'vigorous' capitalism, in which the frenzy of achievement, the constantly shifting and multiple goals and demands, and the incessant demands of work at all times of the day, are burning us out as individuals and social beings. Helga Nowotny (1994), for example, writes about the decline of time for empathy in this new capitalism of 24-hour activity seven days a week and the vastly speeded-up life-styles and intensity of geographic movement. The city – its parks, squares and hostels, its sites of learning and recreation, its centres of socialisation, sociability and debate, its routine and everyday economic activities – has a vital contribution to make in helping us to slow down. There is no inevitability about the need to speed up everything in contemporary life. Indeed, cities such as Modena in Italy and some Dutch cities are now introducing policies to better manage urban time (eg flexible opening times or subsidised childcare services to cater for the needs of working parents) in order to help busy people to recover their personal and social space. The policies we have suggested are very much about the recovery of space and time for personal and civic development, but for all citizens.

If cities are for the many, then it is not for a few to legislate their form in advance. So our vision of such a city is not of a utopia. That suggests a foreseeable endpoint which the whole logic of this piece is an argument against. Rather our vision consists of principles which might allow the inhabitants of British cities to live life more fully. A vision, then, of cities in which potentiality can be realised in ways which can create both wealth and happiness.

There is no obvious gate to heaven.

References

Adonis, A. and Pollard, S. (1997) *A class act: The myths of Britain's classless society*, London: Hamish Hamilton.

Coates, D. (2000) *Models of capitalism. Growth and stagnation in the modern era*, Cambridge: Polity Press.

Comedia (1995) *Park life: Urban parks and social renewal*, London: Comedia.

Dahle, C. (1999) 'Social justice', *Fast Company*, December, pp 284-92.

Davis, M. (1998) *The ecology of fear*, London: Verso.

DTI (Department of Trade and Industry) (1998) *Our competitive future. Building the knowledge-driven economy*, Cm 4167, London: The Stationery Office.

Fleischacker, S. (1998) 'Insignificant communities', in A. Gutmann (ed) *Freedom of association*, Princeton, NJ: Princeton University Press.

Grabher, G. (2000: forthcoming) 'The organisation of creativity: heterarchies in the advertising industry', *Environment and Planning A*.

Healey, P. (1997) *Collaborative planning*, London: Macmillan.

Leadbeater, C. (1999) *Living on thin air*, London: Allen Lane.

Local Futures Group (1999) *The role of the city in London's knowledge-driven information economy*, London: Corporation of London.

McRobbie, A. (1999) *In the culture society*, London: Routledge.

Mare, K. and Engels, F. (1968) 'The Communist Manifesto', in *Selected works*, London: Laurence and Wishart.

Marr, A. (2000) 'Arise, the city state', *The Observer*, 12 March, p 28.

Marx, K. and Engels, F. (1968) 'The Communist Manifesto', in *Selected works*, London: Laurence and Wishart.

Nowotny, H. (1994) *Time. The modern and postmodern experience*, Cambridge: Polity Press.

Peck, J. and Theodore, N. (1999) 'Insecurity in work and welfare: towards a trans-Atlantic model of labour regulation?', Paper presented to the Annual Conference of the Royal Geographical Society/Institute of British Geographers, Leicester, 4–7 January.

Quah, D. (1997) 'Increasingly weightless economies', *Bank of England Quarterly Bulletin*, vol 37, no 1, pp 49–56.

Sandercock, L. (1998) *Towards cosmopolis*, London: Wiley.

Sen, A.K. (1992) *Inequality reexamined*, New York, NY: Russell Sage Foundation.

Sennett, R. (1998) *The corrosion of character*, New York, NY: Norton and Co.

Soper, K. (1998) 'An alternative hedonism', *Radical Philosophy*, no 92, pp 28–38.

Stiglitz, J. (1999) 'Knowledge in the modern economy', in DTI, *The economics of the knowledge-driven economy*, London: DTI.

Tsagarousianou, R., Tambini, D. and C. Bryan (eds) (1998) *Cyberdemocracy*, London: Routledge.

Turok, I. and Edge, N. (1999) *The jobs gap in Britain's cities: Employment loss and labour market consequences*, Bristol/York: The Policy Press/Joseph Rowntree Foundation.

Unger, R.M. (1998) *Democracy realized*, London: Verso.

Urban Task Force (1999a) *Towards an urban renaissance* (The Rogers Report), London: DETR.

Urban Task Force (1999b) 'Executive summary', *Towards an urban renaissance*, London: DETR.

Yuval-Davis, N. (1999) 'What is "transversal politics"?', *Soundings*, vol 12, pp 94–8.